Cavan Man
JOKES

THE BOOK OF
Cavan
Man
JOKES

DES MacHALE

MERCIER PRESS
WHAT YOU NEED TO READ

MERCIER PRESS
Douglas Village, Cork, Ireland
www.mercierpress.ie

Trade enquiries to COLUMBA MERCIER DISTRIBUTION,
55a Spruce Avenue, Stillorgan Industrial Park, Blackrock, Dublin

© Des MacHale, 2006

ISBN: 1 85635 516 0

10 9 8 7 6 5 4 3 2 1

Mercier Press receives financial assistance from
the Arts Council/An Chomhairle Ealaíon

Printed and Bound by ColourBooks Ltd

INTRODUCTION

For many years I inflicted some pain on the inhabitants of Kerry by writing books of Kerry man jokes. Actually I now realise I did them a favour – before my books very few people had heard of Kerry, but now everybody knows about it and the place is booming financially and crawling with tourists. But do I get any thanks? Not a bit of it.

Now I am moving my geographical focus to the county of Cavan and I bet that in ten years time it will be booming too. Maybe even winning All-Ireland football titles (that's the first joke in the book!). Yes, you are reading the opening lines of *The Book of Cavan Man Jokes*, destined to put Cavan on the map and immortalise the county in the annals of Irish history. It's not that Cavan men are mean – it's just that they have short arms and deep pockets! In fact some of my *closest* friends are from Cavan.

To be fair to Kerry men, I received only one complaining letter after I wrote all those books – and that was from a Cork man who was jealous because he hadn't thought of the idea first. I don't expect to receive any hate mail from Cavan men either, because that would involve buying a stamp.

So sit back and enjoy Ireland's latest joke craze – the Cavan man joke. Note that for maximum effect, many of these jokes should be read in an authentic Khavun accent, but don't contact me for lessons – I'm going to be in hiding for the next couple of years!

Des MacHale
Cork, 2006

One Cavan man calls on another and finds him tearing strips of wallpaper off the wall.

'Are you redecorating?' he asks him.

'No,' says the second Cavan man, 'I'm moving house.'

☺   ☺   ☺

Have you heard about the Cavan man who had a brass band at his wedding?

It was on the bride's finger.

☺   ☺   ☺

Ad in a Cavan newspaper:

SECOND-HAND TOMBSTONE FOR SALE.
EXCELLENT BARGAIN
TO ANYONE NAMED O'REILLY

☺   ☺   ☺

A true Cavan man never sends a suit to the dry-cleaners without a pair of socks in every pocket.

☺   ☺   ☺

A Cavan man took his wife to a restaurant and they both ordered dinner. As the wife ate her dinner the Cavan man just sat there looking at his food.

'Is there something the matter with your meal, sir?' a waiter asked him.

'No,' said the Cavan man, 'I'm just waiting for my wife to finish with the teeth.'

☺   ☺   ☺

What is the difference between a Cavan man and a coconut?

You can get a drink out of a coconut.

7

A Cavan man went to London on his honeymoon, but he didn't bring the wife because she had been to London before.

☺   ☺   ☺

An American tourist was being driven by his chauffeur around the north of Ireland when they got lost. So they met a little lad on the road and they asked him where they were.

'I'll tell you if you give me €5,' said the little lad.

'Drive on James,' said the American, 'we're in Cavan.'

☺   ☺   ☺

A Cavan man had a dog for sale. A Dubliner offered him €50 for it while an American offered him €100. Surprisingly, he sold it to the Dubliner. He reckoned the dog could easily find his way back from Dublin but would never manage to swim the Atlantic.

☺   ☺   ☺

Oldest joke in the book: In 1673 a Cavan squire was accosted by a highwayman with a pistol.

'Your money or your life,' said the highwayman.

'Give me a few minutes,' said the Cavan squire, 'I'm thinking it over.'

☺   ☺   ☺

A Cavan man was travelling by train from Dublin to Limerick. As he was buying his ticket at Heuston Station the clerk said 'Change at Limerick Junction'.

'I'll have my change now if you don't mind,' said the Cavan man.

Have you heard about the Cavan man who gave a waiter a tip?

The horse lost.

☺   ☺   ☺

One Cavan man bet another a euro that he could stay underwater longer than him. The police are still searching for the bodies.

☺   ☺   ☺

Why do Cavan men never smoke cigarettes while wearing gloves?

They hate the smell of burning leather.

☺   ☺   ☺

A Cavan man was taking a taxi to the railway station.

'How much will it cost?' he asked the driver.

'€15 sir,' said the driver.

'And how much for my suitcase?'

'That goes absolutely free sir,' said the driver.

'Here, take my case,' said the Cavan man, 'I'll walk to the station.'

☺   ☺   ☺

Cavan schoolchildren never write their names on their schoolbooks – it would kill the resale value.

☺   ☺   ☺

A Dublin man, a Cork man and a Cavan man were invited to a big party. The Dublin man brought a six-pack of Guinness. The Cork man brought a six-pack of Murphy's. The Cavan man brought his brother.

How do you recognise a left-handed Cavan man?
He keeps all his money in his right-hand pocket.

☺   ☺   ☺

A Cavan man had identical twin sons named Juan and Amal. So he had a photo taken of Juan and told people to imagine that Amal looked exactly like his brother. Like the old proverb says, when you've seen Juan, you've seen Amal!

☺   ☺   ☺

A Cork man was up in court, being tried for being drunk and disorderly. The judge aked him where he had bought all the liquor.

'I didn't buy it your honour,' said the Cork man, 'a Cavan man gave it to me.'

'Fourteen days for perjury,' said the judge.

☺   ☺   ☺

The following ad appeared in the 'Lost and Found' columns of a Cavan newspaper:

LOST: A €10 NOTE. SENTIMENTAL VALUE.

☺   ☺   ☺

Have you heard about the Cavan man who found a bottle of cough mixture?

He sat for four hours in the rain in his back garden.

☺   ☺   ☺

A Cavan man had to travel by train to Dublin for a serious heart operation. He bought a single ticket.

☺   ☺   ☺

A little Cavan lad burst into his house and said proudly to his father: 'Daddy, daddy, I ran all the way home behind a bus and saved a euro.'

His father replied, 'You could have done better son. You could have run home behind a taxi and saved €10.'

☺   ☺   ☺

Two Cavan men were out for a walk together when one of them realised he was out of cigarettes. He asked his friend for a match and when it was handed over he searched his pockets and said, 'I seem to have forgotten my cigarettes.'

'In that case,' said the other Cavan man, 'I'll have that match back, because you won't be needing it.'

☺   ☺   ☺

How do you know if you're flying over Cavan?

Locks on the dustbins.

☺   ☺   ☺

Have you heard about the two Cavan burglars who were arrested after a smash and grab raid?

They were caught when they went back for their brick.

☺   ☺   ☺

A Cavan man and his girlfriend had a huge row and it seemed to everyone that the wedding was off. The girl was very upset and took to comfort eating in a big way. Finally to everyone's surprise, they settled their differences and got married. It seems the girl put on so much weight the Cavan man couldn't get the ring off her finger.

Why are Cavan churches circular?

So nobody can hide in the corners during the collection.

☺ ☺ ☺

Have you heard about the Cavan kamikaze pilot?

He crashed his plane in his brother's scrapyard.

☺ ☺ ☺

What is the definition of an optimist?

A fellow who buys something from one Cavan man hoping to sell it to another Cavan man at a profit.

☺ ☺ ☺

A Cavan man was once guilty of false economy. He went to bed early to save electricity but the result was that his wife had twins.

☺ ☺ ☺

DOCTOR: 'You have a very serious illness but there is an operation that will save your life. However, it will cost €1,000.'

CAVAN MAN: 'That's a terrible extravagance doctor. Do you think it's worth it?'

☺ ☺ ☺

Have you heard about the Cavan man who found a corn plaster?

He went out and bought a pair of tight shoes.

☺ ☺ ☺

A Cavan man boasted that he had the most sensitive feet in the world. He could stand on a fifty cent piece and tell if it was heads or tails.

Have you heard about the Cavan footballer who lent the referee a coin for the toss before the match and demanded his whistle as security?

☺ ☺ ☺

Two Cavan men were having dinner together in a Dublin hotel. After the dinner one of the Cavan men was heard to call for the bill.

Next day the newspaper headlines read:

CAVAN VENTRILOQUIST
FOUND MURDERED

☺ ☺ ☺

Why are there no juvenile delinquents in Cavan?

Crime doesn't pay.

☺ ☺ ☺

A beggar stopped a Cavan man in the street and asked for a little help.

'Do you realise where you are?' the Cavan man said to him, 'this is Cavan.'

☺ ☺ ☺

A Cavan man took a holiday in Dublin but returned home after a few days.

'Why did you return so soon?' the lads in the pub asked him.

'I couldn't stand the extravagance of the place,' he told them. 'I'd only been there two days when bang went €5.'

'And what did you spend that kind of money on?'

'I don't rightly remember,' said the Cavan man, 'but it was mostly wine and women.'

How was the Grand Canyon formed?

A Cavan man in America lost a cent.

☺ ☺ ☺

A Cavan man's wife was so unwell he took her to the doctor to be examined.

'It's her tonsils,' said the doctor, 'they will have to come out. Actually that operation should have been done when she was a little girl.'

'That's good news,' said the Cavan man, 'You can send the bill to my father-in-law.'

☺ ☺ ☺

An insurance agent called on a ninety year old Cavan man and asked him if he would like to take out a policy to cover his funeral expenses.

'I don't think so,' said the Cavan man. 'After all, I could be lost at sea.'

☺ ☺ ☺

A Kerry man, a Cork man and a Cavan man were travelling on a jumbo jet when the pilot got into difficulties. In desperation he asked the passengers to do something religious.

The Kerry man recited the Lord's Prayer.

The Cork man sang 'Nearer my God to Thee'.

The Cavan man took his cap off and went around and took up a collection.

☺ ☺ ☺

The police finally picked up the Cavan obscene telephone caller.

He kept reversing the charges.

☺ ☺ ☺

A Cavan man prayed to God for many years that he would win a big prize in the Lotto. Finally, he shouted up to the heavens, 'Lord, just what do I have to do to win the Lotto?'

And the voice of God came booming back: 'well, you could buy a ticket for a start.'

☺ ☺ ☺

On Christmas Eve a Cavan man went behind his house and fired a gun. He then told his children that Santa Claus had committed suicide.

☺ ☺ ☺

A Cavan man's tooth was paining him so he paid a visit to the dentist. As he sat nervously in the dentist's chair he fumbled in his pocket clanking his coins.

'There's no need to pay me in advance,' said the dentist.

'It's not that,' said the Cavan man, 'I'm just counting my money before you put me under the gas.'

☺ ☺ ☺

'I'm sorry to hear your wife died,' said one Cavan man to another.

'You're not nearly as sorry as I am,' said the second Cavan man, 'she had taken hardly any of those expensive pills I had to buy her.'

☺ ☺ ☺

A beggar asked a Cavan man for a euro for a cup of coffee.

'Show me the cup of coffee first,' said the Cavan man.

There was once a very generous Cavan man who liked to donate a lot of money to charity. However, he modestly wanted to remain anonymous so he never even signed his name on the cheques.

☺   ☺   ☺

A ten cent piece rolled out of a Cavan man's pocket and on to a busy city street. As he ran after it he was hit by a bus and killed. The jury returned a verdict of death from natural causes.

☺   ☺   ☺

Have you heard about the Cavan man who threw caution to the winds?

He gave the canary another seed.

☺   ☺   ☺

Have you heard about the Cavan man who gave €100,000 to charity?

Nobody else has either.

☺   ☺   ☺

Why do Cavan men travel first-class on the train?

It's the only way they can avoid people they owe money to.

☺   ☺   ☺

Two Dubliners and a Cavan man went to the pub for a drink.

The first Dubliner stood a round.

The second Dubliner stood a round.

The Cavan man stood around.

☺   ☺   ☺

How do you disperse an angry Cavan mob?

Take up a collection.

☺ ☺ ☺

A Cavan man went to the dentist and was told it would cost €100 to have a tooth extracted.

'That's a lot of money for five minutes' work,' said the Cavan man.

'I can pull it very slowly if you like,' smiled the dentist.

'Look,' said the Cavan man, 'Here's €10. Just loosen it a bit.'

☺ ☺ ☺

A very rich man had a Kerry man, a Cork man and a Cavan man working for him. He promised to divide his fortune among them if each of them put €1,000 in his coffin just in case he needed it on the other side.

When he died the Kerry man tearfully put €1,000 in notes into his coffin.

Similarly the Cork man tearfully put €1,000 in notes into the coffin.

The Cavan man took the €2,000 in notes out of the coffin and put in his cheque for €3,000.

☺ ☺ ☺

A Cavan man was being interviewed by a reporter after his big Lotto win. At the same draw he had won prizes of €2 million and a million euro.

'How do you feel?' the reporter asked him.

'Disappointed,' said the Cavan man, 'I bought a third ticket and it won nothing.'

☺ ☺ ☺

This fellow rang up a Cavan man to ask him if he could borrow €50.

'I'm sorry,' said the Cavan man, 'it's a fierce bad line, I can't hear a word you're saying.'

'Can you lend me €50?' shouted the fellow over the phone.

'I still can't hear a word,' said the Cavan man.

At this stage the operator intervened and said, 'the line is perfectly ok – I can hear him clearly.'

'In that case,' said the Cavan man, 'you lend him the €50.'

☺   ☺   ☺

What do Cavan men do with old razor blades?

They shave with them.

☺   ☺   ☺

As the *Titanic* was sinking it is said that there was a Cavan man rushing round to all the lifeboats shouting frantically, 'is there anyone who wants to buy a genuine diamond ring for £5?'

☺   ☺   ☺

Have you heard about the Cavan man who sued a football club for damages because he was injured while he was a spectator at a big match?

He fell out of the tree he was sitting in.

☺   ☺   ☺

A Cavan man went into a shop to buy a suitcase.

'Will I wrap it for you sir?' asked the assistant.

'No,' said the Cavan man, 'just put the string and paper inside.'

☺   ☺   ☺

A Cavan man had just got engaged and handed over a beautiful ring to his girlfriend.

'Ooh,' she gasped, 'is it a real diamond?'

'If it's not,' said the Cavan man, 'I've just been done out of €10.'

☺ ☺ ☺

Two Cavan men were on their way home from the pub when they were attacked by a mugger with a gun who demanded their money.

'Here's that €20 I owe you,' said one Cavan man to the other.

☺ ☺ ☺

Why do Cavan men have such a great sense of humour?

Because it's a gift.

☺ ☺ ☺

Two Cavan men were up in court charged with being drunk and disorderly.

The judge asked the policeman why he suspected they were drunk.

'Well your honour,' said the policeman, 'one of them was throwing away €20 notes and the other was picking them up and handing them back to him.'

☺ ☺ ☺

A Kerry man, a Cork man and a Cavan man went on a pub crawl one night. The Kerry man spent €50, the Cork man €60 and the Cavan man spent a very enjoyable night indeed.

☺ ☺ ☺

One Cavan man sent another Cavan man a letter but he put his own name on the front of it and his friend's name and address on the back. Then he posted the letter without a stamp. When the letter was delivered to his house he refused to pay the postage due so the letter was sent to his friend – the name and address on the back.

☺   ☺   ☺

A Cavan man won a million euro on the Lotto so he rushed round to his parents' house and told them the good news.

'And guess what?' he said to them. 'I'm going to give each of you €100.'

His father took him aside and said, 'son, there's something I've been meaning to tell you. Many years ago, when I first met your mother, money was in very short supply and to tell you the truth, we didn't have enough money to get married, so we never did.'

'My God,' said the Cavan man, 'you know what that makes me?'

'Yes,' said the father, 'and a mean one at that.'

☺   ☺   ☺

A Kerry man, a Cork man and a Cavan man went into a restaurant and ordered a bowl of soup. When the soup arrived there was a fly in each of the bowls.

The Kerry man ate up his soup because he was very hungry.

The Cork man complained to the manager.

The Cavan man carefully removed the fly with his spoon and wrung it dry before he disposed of it.

Have you heard about the Cavan man who married a girl born on 29 February?

He reckoned he would have to buy her a birthday present only once every four years.

☺ ☺ ☺

A Cavan man was very hard of hearing but when he went to buy a hearing aid, he found they were a fierce price altogether. So he bought a piece of string and let it hang out of his ear. He found people spoke much louder to him.

☺ ☺ ☺

A Cavan man in a railway station was in a very distressed condition.

'What is the matter?' an official asked him.

'I think I've lost my wallet,' said the Cavan man, 'and I've searched in every one of my pockets except one.'

'And why don't you search in that pocket?' the official continued.

'Because if it's not in that pocket,' said the Cavan man, 'I'm going to drop down dead.'

☺ ☺ ☺

A Dubliner on holiday in Cavan saw a little lad get into difficulty while swimming in a lake so he dived in fully clothed and rescued him. The little lad's mother rushed up to him and said, 'are you the man who rescued my wee lad?'

'Yes,' said the Dubliner modestly, 'but there's no need for a reward.'

'It's not that,' said the Cavan woman, 'where's his cap?'

There was a bit of a row at a Cavan cinema the other night. Two Cavan men were trying to get in to see the show on just one ticket claiming they were half brothers.

☺   ☺   ☺

This fellow heard a knock at his door one night and when he opened it he found a Cavan man there taking up a collection for a poor widow woman who was about to be evicted for non-payment of rent on her little house. So the fellow threw €10 into the box and asked the Cavan man if he was one of the woman's neighbours.

'No,' he replied, 'I'm her landlord.'

☺   ☺   ☺

Have you heard about the Cavan man who counted his money in front of the mirror so he wouldn't cheat himself?

☺   ☺   ☺

Have you heard about the Cavan man who went to a fancy dress party dressed as Napoleon?

He wanted to keep his hand on his wallet at all times.

☺   ☺   ☺

A Cavan man wrote to his girlfriend:
My Darling,
I love you so much. I would climb the highest mountain, swim the deepest sea and crawl through raging fires to be by your side.

Your loving Phelim.

P.S. I'll be over to see you Monday night if it's not raining.

A Cavan man went into a shop to buy an apple and was standing at the counter counting his change. After he'd counted his change for the fifth time, the annoyed shopkeeper said, 'what's the matter, haven't I given you the correct change?'

'Yes,' said the Cavan man, 'but only just.'

☺ ☺ ☺

There was a collision between two taxis in Cavan. Fifteen people were seriously injured. Twenty others escaped with cuts and bruises.

☺ ☺ ☺

What does a Cavan man put on his roof at Christmas?

A parking meter.

☺ ☺ ☺

At an auction in Cavan a rich businessman lost his wallet which was stuffed with banknotes. He asked the auctioneer to make an announcement that there would be a reward for the safe return of the wallet. So the auctioneer announced: 'A wallet has been lost and there will be a reward of €50 for its safe return.'

'I'll give €100,' rang out a Cavan accent from the back of the room.

☺ ☺ ☺

Why are there so few Cavan opticians and so many Cavan dentists?

People have thirty-two teeth but only two eyes.

☺ ☺ ☺

A Cavan man woke up one morning to find his wife dead beside him in the bed. So he shouted downstairs to the maid: 'You need boil only one egg this morning.'

☺   ☺   ☺

A Cavan man took up golf so he went round to the golf course to have a game. A young lad offered his services as a caddy, so the Cavan man said to him, 'are you good at finding lost golf balls?'

'Very good,' said the lad.

'Well,' said the Cavan man, 'find one and we'll start.'

☺   ☺   ☺

Have you heard about the Cavan man who decided not to buy a new atlas until world affairs had settled down a bit?

☺   ☺   ☺

A priest noticed that his collection one Sunday contained two one cent pieces so before the sermon he joked to his congregation: 'I see we have two Cavan men with us today.'

A voice from the back of the church rang out: 'there are three of them, father'.

So the priest announced that there would be a second collection with a minimum contribution of €1.

At this, one of the Cavan men fainted and the other two carried him out.

☺   ☺   ☺

Why did a Cavan man buy a black and white dog?

He thought the licence would be cheaper.

Two Cavan men went into a restaurant and had a ploughman's lunch. The ploughman was furious.

☺   ☺   ☺

Have you heard about the Cavan man who was going on a hot date so he decided to douse himself in toilet water?

Unfortunately he banged his head on the seat.

☺   ☺   ☺

A Cavan man lay dying and was listening to his family discussing how to save expenses on the funeral.

'Maybe we could get a cheap coffin,' said one son, 'and carry it to save the expense of a hearse.'

'Better still,' said the Cavan man with his last breath, 'give me my trousers and I'll walk to the cemetery.'

☺   ☺   ☺

A Cavan man applied to join the anti-tipping society but when he heard that the annual subscription was a euro decided that it would be cheaper to continue tipping.

☺   ☺   ☺

A woman's husband died and that very afternoon there was a knock on the door and when she opened it there was a Cavan man standing there.

'Is your husband in?' he asked her.

'I'm sorry,' she wept, 'he passed away this morning.'

'Did he mention anything about a pot of green paint before he departed?' said the Cavan man.

How do you recognise a Cavan café?

Forks in the sugar bowl.

☺ ☺ ☺

A rich man was very ill and needed several blood transfusions. The only person in the country who had the same blood type was a Cavan man who generously donated enough blood for three transfusions.

After the first transfusion he sent the Cavan man a present of €1,000.

After the second transfusion he sent him a present of €500.

After the third transfusion he just thanked him.

☺ ☺ ☺

Two Cavan men met each other after an interval of thirty years.

'It'll be great to have a drink together after all that time,' said one.

'Yes,' said the other, 'but remember, it's your shout.'

☺ ☺ ☺

Why did the old 50p pieces have that peculiar shape?

So you could get them out of a Cavan man's hand with a spanner.

☺ ☺ ☺

A doctor rang his Cavan patient.

'I'm afraid that cheque you gave me came back,' said the doctor.

'So did my arthritis, doc,' said the Cavan man.

A Cavan man received a lot of bills every month so he divided them into three categories:

Category 1: Bills to be paid at once
Category 2: Bills that would be paid some day
Category 3: Bills that would never be paid.

To one company who sent him a polite reminder he replied:

Dear Sir,
Because of the friendly tone of your letter, I have decided to promote you from Category Three to Category Two.

To another company who threatened legal proceedings he replied:

Dear Sir,
Because of the unfriendly tone of your letter, I have decided to penalise you by not putting you in the draw for the next three months.

☺   ☺   ☺

A Cavan man wrote this letter to his ex-girlfriend:
My darling,
I am sorry about the big row we had. I realise now that I was totally in the wrong and you were right. I cannot live without you and I love you to bits. Can we get together again, forget our differences and be happy together?
Your loving Liam.
P.S. Congratulations on winning the Lottery.

☺   ☺   ☺

Cavan men hate to part with banknotes once they've memorised the serial numbers.

☺   ☺   ☺

A Cavan man's wife had a temperature of 105 degrees. So he put her in the cellar to heat the house.

☺   ☺   ☺

Once upon a time there were three Cavan men.

The first wouldn't give you a slide if he owned the Alps.

The second wouldn't tell you the time if he had three watches.

The third wouldn't give you a light if his trousers were on fire.

☺   ☺   ☺

This Cavan farmer had a herd of prize cows so he hired a premium bull from the Department of Agriculture to service them. After two weeks there was no sign of the bull being returned so the department dispatched one of their inspectors up to Cavan to see what the problem was.

He called at the farmer's house but there was nobody in. In desperation he toured the fields until he finally came across his man. The farmer had the bull hitched to a plough and was whipping him around the field shouting, 'Get along outa that ye bugger ye; that'll teach you there's more to life than romance.'

☺   ☺   ☺

You can always recognise a Cavan restaurant. They heat the knives so you can't use too much butter.

☺   ☺   ☺

How much can a Cavan man drink?

Any given amount.

☺   ☺   ☺

In Cavan they have invented a sure fire cure for seasickness.

You lean over the side of the ship with a euro coin between your teeth.

☺   ☺   ☺

'Stand behind your lover woman,' shouted a Cavan man who had come home and surprised his wife with another man. 'I'm going to shoot you both.'

☺   ☺   ☺

A Cavan man was stopped by a beggar who told him that he hadn't eaten a square meal in three days.

So the Cavan man gave him a cream cracker.

☺   ☺   ☺

Have you heard about the three Cavan men who went for a big night out on the town?

They ordered a bottle of lemonade and three straws.

☺   ☺   ☺

A Cavan man promised his wife a surprise for her birthday. So he jumped out from behind a door and shouted 'boo'.

☺   ☺   ☺

You can always tell a stranger in a Cavan pub.

He sometimes puts his drink down.

Two burglars burgled a Cavan house one night and afterwards were counting their loot.

'We didn't do too badly,' said one, 'we have €300.'

'But,' said the other, 'we had €500 going in.'

☺ ☺ ☺

A Cavan man won a million euro in the Lottery.

'What are we going to do with the begging letters?' asked his wife.

'Keep sending them out,' said the Cavan man, 'keep sending them out.'

☺ ☺ ☺

A little lad swallowed a ten cent coin and two doctors tried in vain to get him to cough it up. Just as they were about to operate, a Cavan man rushed up and did a quick manipulation on the lad and out popped the coin. It only goes to show a Cavan man can get money out of anyone.

☺ ☺ ☺

Two Cavan men on holiday at the seaside hired a rowing boat for an hour for a pleasure cruise. After half an hour, when they were on the open sea, it began to pour with rain, the wind howled and there was thunder and lightning.

'Do you know,' said one of them to the other, 'I'll be glad when the hour is up and we can go back ashore.'

☺ ☺ ☺

A doctor told a Cavan man that his wife needed some sea air.

She awoke next morning to find him waving a kipper over and back in front of her.

A Cavan man spent a day in Dublin – and that's all he spent.

☺   ☺   ☺

What is the difference between a Cavan man and a canoe?

A canoe sometimes tips.

☺   ☺   ☺

A Cavan man went on a pilgrimage to the Holy Land and very much wanted to take a boat across the Sea of Galilee. So he asked a boatman how much it would cost and was horrified to hear the fare was $50.

'That's an awful lot for a short trip,' he said to the boatman.

'But,' said the boatman, 'this is where Jesus walked on the water.'

'At those prices,' said the Cavan man, 'I'm not surprised he walked.'

☺   ☺   ☺

Have you heard about the generous Cavan man who offered a prize of a million dollars for the first person to swim the Atlantic?

☺   ☺   ☺

A Cavan man found a perfectly good crutch so he went home and broke his wife's leg.

☺   ☺   ☺

Have you heard about the lucky Cavan man who was always finding money under plates in restaurants?

A fellow fell in love with a Cavan girl so he went to her father to ask for her hand in marriage.

'Would you marry my daughter,' asked the father, 'even if she didn't have a penny to her name?'

'I would sir,' said the fellow eagerly.

'Then away with you,' said the father, 'we don't want a fool like you in the family.'

☺   ☺   ☺

A Cavan fisherman had a very successful day's fishing so in the evening he pressed something into the gillie's hand for a drink. It was a teabag.

☺   ☺   ☺

Have you heard about the Cavan man who applied for a no-claims bonus on his life insurance policy?

☺   ☺   ☺

A famous Cavan businessman was teaching his little son the tricks of the trade.

As they were on a country walk together the lad said, 'why are you such a famous businessman, dad?'

'Let me show you son – stand on top of that gate,' he said, indicating an old gate over a dirty muddy pool. 'Now jump son, and your daddy will catch you.'

So the lad did as he was told but at the last moment the father pulled back and the son fell flat into the muddy pool, face first.

'Now that's the first rule of business, son,' said the Cavan man. 'Never trust anybody – not even your own father.'

☺   ☺   ☺

A Cavan man went to a football match and was asked if the gate was big.

'The biggest I ever climbed over,' he replied.

☺   ☺   ☺

A Cavan man went into a barber shop and asked how much a haircut cost.

'€15,' said the barber.

'And how much for a shave?'

'€10,' said the barber.

'Shave my head,' said the Cavan man.

☺   ☺   ☺

A Cavan man was working on a building site when his jacket fell into an open sewer. Without a moment's hesitation he dived in after it and fished it out.

'What was the point of doing that?' the foreman asked, 'even with dry-cleaning, you could never wear that jacket again.'

'But,' said the Cavan man, 'me sangwiches were in the pocket.'

☺   ☺   ☺

A Cavan man went into a bar and ordered a glass of whiskey.

After he had drunk it he was about to walk out when the bar owner said to him, 'excuse me, you didn't pay for that drink.'

'Did you pay for it?' asked the Cavan man.

'Well, yes I did,' said the bar owner.

'Then there's no point both of us paying for it, is there?' said the Cavan man as he walked out leaving the bar owner in a very confused condition.

☺   ☺   ☺

A Cavan man came home one night and said to his wife, 'get your coat on.'

'Oh, are we going out together?' she asked excitedly.

'No,' said the Cavan man, 'I'm going to the pub and I'm turning off the central heating.'

☺ ☺ ☺

A Cavan man got run over by a brewery lorry.

It was the first time in years that the drinks had been on him.

☺ ☺ ☺

Have you heard about the Cavan man who had a hip replacement operation?

He asked the surgeon if he could have the bone for the dog.

☺ ☺ ☺

A Scottish beggar came to live in Cavan. He starved to death.

☺ ☺ ☺

Why do Cavan men always have double glazing in their houses?

So the children can't hear the chimes of the ice cream van passing by.

☺ ☺ ☺

A Cavan man bought his girlfriend lipstick – the Cavan present. He got most of it back.

☺ ☺ ☺

And the Lord said to the blind man:

'You can see,' and the blind man could see.

And the Lord said to the deaf man:

'You can hear,' and the deaf man could hear.

And the Lord said to the Cavan man:

'You can walk,' but the Cavan man shouted back, 'keep away from me, I have a disability pension.'

☺   ☺   ☺

A Cavan man was going to Dublin on a day trip so he was saying goodbye to his little son.

'Take care now,' he told him, 'and be sure to take your glasses off when you're not looking at anything.'

☺   ☺   ☺

A young girl asked a Cavan man for a contribution for the church – 'money for the Lord', as she put it.

'How old are you, girl?' he asked her.

'Sixteen,' she replied.

'Well, I'm eighty,' he said to her. 'I'm bound to see the Lord before you do and I'll give him the money myself'.

☺   ☺   ☺

Have you heard about the Cavan man whose horse swallowed a euro coin?

He's been riding backwards ever since.

Sign in a Cavan garage:
  THE MAN WHO LENDS TOOLS IS OUT

☺   ☺   ☺

A Cavan man has decided to have one of those cut price funerals.

They just loosen the earth and you sink in by yourself.

☺   ☺   ☺

A man was driving from Donegal to Dublin in a Mercedes when he spotted a Cavan man hitching a lift so he stopped and picked him up.

'I won a ticket for the All-Ireland final in a raffle,' said the Cavan man, 'and I'll be staying with the married sister, so it won't cost me a penny. Would you like a mint?'

'Yes,' said the driver, whereupon the Cavan man pulled a mint from his pocket, dusted off the fluff and debris and handed it to him. The driver swallowed his pride and the mint.

They pulled in for petrol and the driver said to his passenger, 'would you like a sandwich and a can of Coke?'

'Yes,' said the Cavan man and quickly consumed his free meal.

As they neared Dublin the Cavan man said, 'would you like another mint?'

'No,' said the driver quickly, 'I'm quite full, thank you,' and he added a little sarcastically, 'you're very generous with the mints.'

'Well,' said the Cavan man, 'when yer out, yer out.'

☺   ☺   ☺

How was copper wire invented?

Two Cavan men fighting over a penny.

☺   ☺   ☺

A Cavan man visiting London lost a pound coin, so naturally he reported the incident to the police.

Later that day he came upon hundreds of workmen excavating for an extension to the Underground.

'My, but the police are very thorough in this city,' he said to himself.

☺ ☺ ☺

What is the most popular gift in Cavan at Christmas?

Homing pigeons.

☺ ☺ ☺

They took a Cavan man out of the lake the other day. They knew he was a goner because they searched through all his pockets looking for identification and he didn't even move.

☺ ☺ ☺

Cavan men are famous for keeping the Sabbath and anything else they can lay their hands on.

☺ ☺ ☺

Have you heard about the Cavan football referee who at the beginning of a match tossed a coin and lost it in the mud?

He immediately abandoned the game and set both teams looking for it.

☺ ☺ ☺

Have you heard about the Cavan man who went from door to door taking up a collection for the widow of the unknown soldier?

A Cavan man came across an overturned car at a level crossing. Beside the car lay a man moaning and covered in blood.

'Has there been an accident?' asked the Cavan man.

'Yes,' groaned the man, 'call for a doctor and an ambulance.'

'Have the police and insurance people arrived yet?'

'No, no,' groaned the man, 'please get medical help.'

'Move over,' said the Cavan man, 'and let me lie down beside you.'

☺ ☺ ☺

Archaeologists on a dig in Cavan uncovered a penny dated 1737 BC. Nearby they found three skeletons on their hands and knees.

☺ ☺ ☺

A fellow wanted to marry a Cavan man's daughter but couldn't pluck up the courage to propose. Finally, he hit on a plan.

'How would you like,' he asked the Cavan man, 'to find a sure fire way of saving money?'

☺ ☺ ☺

How do you take a census in Cavan?

Throw a ten cent coin in the street.

☺ ☺ ☺

Why are Cavan men such good golfers?

They realise that the fewer times they hit the ball the longer it will last.

Two men came to a Cavan man's door collecting for the local swimming pool. So he gave them a bucket of water.

☺ ☺ ☺

A Cavan man was at home one evening when his wife rushed in and told him there was a strange cow in the garden.

'What will I do with her?' she asked.

'What a silly question,' said the Cavan man. 'Milk her and turn her out.'

☺ ☺ ☺

CAVAN MAN: Could I hire a horse please?
CLERK: Certainly sir. Any particular kind of horse?
CAVAN MAN: A long one – there are five of us.

☺ ☺ ☺

What is the Cavan man's dilemma?

Whether to take longer steps to save shoe leather or shorter steps to avoid the strain on the stitches of his underpants.

☺ ☺ ☺

One Monday morning a Cavan shopkeeper was surprised to have two toilet rolls returned with the following note: Could you please refund the money on these toilet rolls? The cousins from Dublin didn't come for the weekend after all.

☺ ☺ ☺

A beggar called at a Cavan man's door and told him he hadn't eaten anything in three days.

'Go on,' said the Cavan man, 'force yourself.'

A Cavan man owned a fish and chip shop and one night a fellow rushed in saying he was in a desperate fix and needed to borrow €100.

'I'd love to lend it to you,' said the Cavan man, 'but I'm afraid I can't because of an arrangement I have with the bank.'

'What's that?' asked the fellow.

'They don't sell fish and chips,' said the Cavan man, ' and I don't lend money.'

☺   ☺   ☺

A Cavan woman went out and lost her handbag containing all her jewellery and a pearl necklace given to her by her husband as a birthday present.

She told the police, 'it's not so much the loss of the jewellery I mind, but there was a €5 note in that handbag.'

☺   ☺   ☺

PSYCHIATRIST TO A CAVAN MAN When did you first get this feeling that you wanted to treat your friends?

☺   ☺   ☺

A Cavan man found an old telephone directory. It made an ideal address book. He just crossed out the names of all the people he didn't know.

☺   ☺   ☺

Have you heard about the Cavan man who attached a mirror to his dog's feeding bowl to make the poor animal feel he was getting two bones for his dinner?

☺   ☺   ☺

A Cavan farmer won his choice of two hats in a raffle – a felt one and a straw one. He chose the straw one – 'Sure, it'll be a mouthful for the donkey when I'm finished with it.'

☺ ☺ ☺

This Cavan man went to his doctor claiming to be suffering from terrible loss of memory and couldn't remember anything from one minute to the next.

'What do you think I should do, doctor?' he asked him.

'Well,' said the doctor, 'you can pay me in advance for one thing.'

☺ ☺ ☺

A Cavan man went into a shop and asked for a cheap coat hanger.

'Certainly, sir,' said the shop assistant. 'Here's one for fifty cent.'

'Don't you have anything cheaper?' asked the Cavan man.

'Yes,' said the disgusted assistant, 'a nail'.

☺ ☺ ☺

How do you get a Cavan man onto the roof of a pub?

Tell him the drinks are on the house.

☺ ☺ ☺

A Cavan man was in a taxi when the brakes failed.

'Help,' said the driver, 'we're going to crash.'

'Well, for God's sake,' said the Cavan man, 'turn off the meter and hit something cheap.'

A Cavan man was due for a medical examination and the doctor told him to bring a generous urine sample with him. The Cavan man arrived up at the doctor's surgery carrying a whole bucket full.

'My God,' said the doctor, 'you didn't carry that through the streets, did you?'

'I had to,' said the Cavan man, 'they wouldn't let me on the bus.'

When the results of the test arrived, the Cavan man announced to his wife, 'good news, you and I and the kids, grandma, and the dog and cat are all in perfect shape.'

☺   ☺   ☺

A Cavan man found a €50 note. Before he handed it back to the owner, he had it changed into five €10 notes.

☺   ☺   ☺

A Cavan chemistry teacher was conducting an experiment in front of his class.

'Now listen carefully boys,' he said. 'I'm going to drop this €2 coin into this beaker of sulphuric acid. Will it dissolve or not?'

'No it won't sir,' said the class joker.

'How do you know?' the teacher asked.

'Because if it was going to dissolve,' smiled the boy, 'you wouldn't put it into the acid.'

☺   ☺   ☺

DINER: I'm sorry waiter, I have only just enough money to pay my bill. I have nothing left over for a tip.

CAVAN WAITER: Let me add up that bill for you again sir.

Have you heard about the Cavan man who told his children that the gas meter was a savings bank?

☺ ☺ ☺

Why is Monaghan like a pregnant cow?
    They're both near Cavan.

☺ ☺ ☺

What is a sure sign of summer?
    When a Cavan man throws his Christmas tree away.

☺ ☺ ☺

Ad in a Cavan newspaper:
    MAN WHO HAS LOST HIS LEFT LEG
    WISHES TO CONTACT MAN
    WHO HAS LOST HIS RIGHT LEG
    AND TAKES A SIZE NINE SHOE.

☺ ☺ ☺

Why do Cavan men always travel second class on the train?
    There is no third class.

☺ ☺ ☺

If you call unexpectedly on a Cavan farmer, what do you find?
    He's eating his dinner out of a drawer.

☺ ☺ ☺

Why do Cavan men rarely smoke pipes?
    If they're smoking their own tobacco, they cannot enjoy it thinking of the expense.

    If they're smoking someone else's tobacco, the pipe is jammed so tight, it won't draw.

A Cavan man heard about a doctor who charged €50 for the first visit but only €30 for every subsequent visit. So he waltzed into the doctor's surgery and announced: 'Here I am again, Doc.'

'Just keep up the treatment I prescribed the last time,' said the doctor, who was also a Cavan man.

☺   ☺   ☺

A Cavan man went on a date and took his girlfriend home in a taxi. She was so beautiful he could hardly keep his eyes on the meter.

As he was leaving her at her home and getting on his bike she said: 'Be very careful now going home. I'd hate anyone to attack you and steal all the money you didn't spend on me tonight.'

☺   ☺   ☺

How do you recognise a Cavan house?

The doormat is hung up in the hall to save wear and tear.

☺   ☺   ☺

A Cavan man used to save money by pushing his car everywhere. Passers-by used to think he was broken down and help him push.

☺   ☺   ☺

This Cavan man was out for an evening when he met a girl who said she would do anything for a €100.

'Anything?' asked the Cavan man.

'Anything,' answered the girl.

'Right,' said the Cavan man, 'come home with me and paint the house.'

Headline in a Dublin newspaper:
BED COLLAPSES IN CITY HOTEL –
THIRTEEN CAVAN MEN INJURED

☺   ☺   ☺

In a Cavan village there was a young lad noted for his simplicity. Tourists would offer him the choice between a shiny new €2 coin and a battered old €5 note. He would ponder and ponder and finally choose the shiny coin. He became quite a tourist attraction and whole busloads would stop to watch him and laugh at him.

Finally the local schoolmaster took him aside and said, 'you're a big lad now and I hate to see all those people making a fool of you. That battered note is over twice as valuable as the shiny coin.'

'Oh, I know that,' said the Cavan lad, 'but if I ever choose the note, nobody would ever offer me the coin again.'

☺   ☺   ☺

What is the difference between a tightrope and a Cavan man?

A tightrope sometimes gives.

☺   ☺   ☺

A Cavan man bought a toilet brush because he was told they didn't wear out. But it didn't work out very well. After a few months he went back to using paper again.

☺   ☺   ☺

What do you call a Cavan man's boomerang that won't come back?

A stick.

There is a great demand for thimbles in Cavan. They use them for standing each other a whiskey.

☺ ☺ ☺

Every Cavan man's fantasy is to have three women at the same time – one cleaning, one washing and one earning.

☺ ☺ ☺

Have you heard about the Cavan man who died of starvation?

He couldn't bear to eat because he had just paid €40 to have his teeth cleaned.

☺ ☺ ☺

A Cavan man and his wife came out of the pub one night and he said to her, 'will we walk or take a taxi?'

'Let's take a taxi, love,' she replied, 'don't be so Scottish.'

☺ ☺ ☺

A man went to a Cavan marriage counsellor and told him that he could not decide between two women – a beautiful penniless young girl and an ugly widow with lots of money.

'I think you should marry the young girl,' said the Cavan man.

'You're right,' said the fellow, 'I will follow your advice.'

'In that case,' said the Cavan man, 'could you give me the widow's address?'

☺ ☺ ☺

DOCTOR: I'll examine you for €40.
CAVAN MAN: Good luck to you doctor, and if you can find them I'll give you ten of them.

☺   ☺   ☺

A Cavan man found a bottle of cough mixture so he sent his children out to play in their pyjamas in the snow.

☺   ☺   ☺

Why do Cavan men have rubber-lined pockets?
    So they can bring soup home from restaurants.

☺   ☺   ☺

How do you know Cavan are playing in Croke Park?
    They sell only four programmes – one for each stand.

☺   ☺   ☺

How many Cavan men does it take to change a lightbulb?
    None. Sure the dark is fine.

☺   ☺   ☺

Two Cavan man travelled by boat and train to London.
    'That was a long and exhausting journey,' said one to the other.
    'So it should be,' said his companion. 'Look at the money it cost us.'

☺   ☺   ☺

The Bumper Book of Kerryman Jokes is the biggest and best collection of Kerryman jokes ever published. It contains hundreds of jokes, riddles, one-liners, stories and inventions.

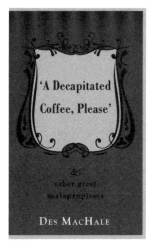

'*A Decapitated Coffee Please*' contains a large collection of hilarious bloopers and howlers.

'... a truly bonkers collection of malapropisms and misnomers, lovingly brought together by Des MacHale ...'

The Times